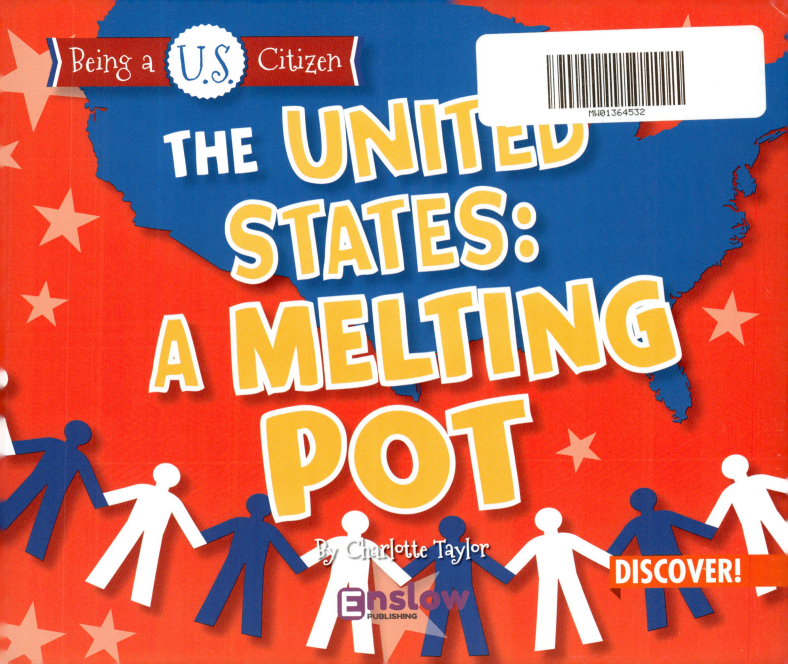

Please visit our website, www.enslow.com. For a free color catalog of all our high-quality books, call toll free 1-800-398-2504 or fax 1-877-980-4454.

Library of Congress Cataloging-in-Publication Data

Names: Taylor, Charlotte, 1978– author.
Title: The United States : A Melting Pot / Charlotte Taylor.
Description: New York : Enslow Publishing, [2021] | Series: Being a U.S. citizen | Includes index.
Identifiers: LCCN 2019050639 | ISBN 9781978517578 (library binding) | ISBN 9781978517554 (paperback) | ISBN 9781978517561 (6-pack) | ISBN 9781978517585 (ebook)
Subjects: LCSH: United States—Ethnic relations—Juvenile literature. | United States—Race relations—Juvenile literature. | Ethnicity—United States—Juvenile literature. | Group identity—United States—Juvenile literature. | Multiculturalism—Juvenile literature. | Cultural pluralism—Juvenile literature. | Emigration and immigration—Juvenile literature. | Citizenship—Juvenile literature.
Classification: LCC E184.A1 T393 2021 | DDC 305.800973—dc23
LC record available at https://lccn.loc.gov/2019050639

Published in 2021 by
Enslow Publishing
101 West 23rd Street, Suite #240
New York, NY 10011

Copyright © 2021 Enslow Publishing

Designer: Laura Bowen
Editor: Megan Quick

Photo credits: Cover, pp. 1, 4 (USA) arnica montana/Shutterstock.com; cover, pp. 1, 8 (people chain) Cienpies Design/Shutterstock.com; p. 5 FatCamera/E+/Getty Images; p. 6 Sarunyu_foto/Shutterstock.com; p. 7 Popperfoto/Contributor/Popperfoto/Getty Images; p. 9 Drew Angerer/Staff/Getty Images News/Getty Images; p. 11 Zurijeta/iStock.com; p. 12 FARBAI/Shutterstock.com; p. 13 thesomegirl/iStock.com; p. 14 (child clothing) Neda Sadreddin/Shutterstock.com; p. 14 (child face) ann131313/Shutterstock.com; p. 15 CraigRJD/iStock/Getty Images Plus/Getty Images; p. 16 VectorMine/Shutterstock.com; p. 17 saiyood/iStock.com; p. 18 vladwel/Shutterstock.com; p. 19 monkeybusinessimages/iStock.com; p. 21 skynesher/E+/Getty Images.

Portions of this work were originally authored by Joanna Anderson and published as *The Many People of America*. All new material in this edition was authored by Charlotte Taylor.

All rights reserved. No part of this book may be reproduced in any form without permission in writing from the publisher, except by a reviewer.

Printed in the United States of America

Some of the images in this book illustrate individuals who are models. The depictions do not imply actual situations or events.

CPSIA compliance information: Batch #BS20ENS: For further information contact Enslow Publishing, New York, New York, at 1-800-398-2504.

CONTENTS

Free to Be Different 4
Coming to America 6
Many Voices 10
Let's Eat! 12
All Dressed Up .14
Having Faith 16
When We Don't Agree 18
America's Future 20
Words to Know 22
For More Information 23
Index 24

Boldface words appear in Words to Know.

FREE TO BE DIFFERENT

The United States has many different kinds of people. They do not all look the same. They do not all dress or speak the same way. But they are all Americans. In America, every person has the right to be different.

OUR DIFFERENCES MAKE OUR COUNTRY INTERESTING!

COMING TO AMERICA

Long ago, people started moving to America because they wanted a better life. Some people in their countries did not want them to be different. America seemed like a safe place for them to be happy and free.

YEARS AGO, MANY PEOPLE CAME TO AMERICA BY BOAT.

Today, many people still come to America from other countries. There is a lot of **diversity** in America. This means there are lots of differences among the people. Their hair, skin, and eyes may all look different. America's diversity makes it special.

MANY VOICES

The United States does not have an **official** language. Most Americans speak English. But some people speak the language of the country where they used to live. Others speak a different language because their family members came from another country.

Hello!

Ciao!

Americans may speak English as well as other languages.

LET'S EAT!

The United States has many different kinds of food. When people came from other countries, they brought their foods with them. You can eat these foods at **restaurants** or at home. Trying new foods helps you learn about different people and places.

IN AMERICA, WE HAVE FOODS FROM AROUND THE WORLD. YUM!

ALL DRESSED UP

The way that we dress says a lot about who we are. Americans dress in all different ways! Some people choose to dress in **traditional** clothes. They are Americans, but they are still proud of the countries they came from.

SOME AMERICANS WEAR TRADITIONAL CLOTHING ON SPECIAL HOLIDAYS.

HAVING FAITH

Americans have all different **faiths**. These are the things that they believe in. Some people go to special places to **worship**. A person's faith can be an important part of who they are. Every American has the right to believe whatever they want.

PARENTS MAY TEACH THEIR CHILDREN ABOUT THEIR FAITH.

WHEN WE DON'T AGREE

Americans have lots of different ideas about everything. They also have the right to say what they believe. Sometimes, they disagree. That is OK. We all have a voice. But even when we don't agree, we should show **respect** for others.

TALKING TOGETHER CAN HELP PEOPLE UNDERSTAND EACH OTHER.

AMERICA'S FUTURE

American life mixes the old and the new. We remember where we came from. But we also look ahead. In America, we are free to become who we want to be. We respect differences in others. This makes our country great!

AMERICA'S PEOPLE ARE ALL SPECIAL IN THEIR OWN WAY.

WORDS TO KNOW

diversity The state of having different people in a community.

faith A strong belief in something.

official Having the support of a group.

respect A feeling that someone is important and should be treated in a fair way.

restaurant A place to buy and eat a meal.

traditional Having to do with something from the past that has been used for a long time.

worship To honor as a god.

FOR MORE INFORMATION

Books

Ringgold, Faith. *We Came to America.* New York, NY: Alfred A. Knopf, 2016.

Scillian, Devin. *A Is for America: An American Alphabet.* New York, NY: Weigl, 2017.

Websites

Ducksters: Ellis Island
www.ducksters.com/history/us_1800s/ellis_island.php
Find out about the place where many people began their new lives in America.

Scholastic: Meet Young Immigrants
teacher.scholastic.com/activities/immigration/young_immigrants/
Meet young people who have just moved to America.

Publisher's note to educators and parents: Our editors have carefully reviewed these websites to ensure that they are suitable for students. Many websites change frequently, however, and we cannot guarantee that a site's future contents will continue to meet our high standards of quality and educational value. Be advised that students should be closely supervised whenever they access the internet.

INDEX

clothing/dress, 4, 14

differences, 4, 6, 8, 10, 12, 14, 16, 18, 20

disagreements, 18

diversity, 8

English, 10

faiths, 16

foods, 12

freedom, 6, 20

language, 10

pride, 14

respect, 18, 20

restaurants, 12

traditional clothes, 14

worship, 16